The Mind Reset

The Mind Reset

Matthew Petchinsky

The Mind Reset: Unlocking Your Inner Peace in a Chaotic World
By: Matthew Petchinsky

Introduction

In the chaos of modern life, mental clutter has become an insidious thief, silently robbing us of our peace, productivity, and overall well-being. Whether it's the incessant hum of daily responsibilities, unresolved emotional baggage, or the ever-present barrage of information from the digital world, mental clutter can leave us feeling overwhelmed, disconnected, and fatigued. This introduction delves into why mental clutter blocks peace and explores the transformative power of a mental reset.

Why Mental Clutter Blocks Peace

Mental clutter manifests as a tangled web of thoughts, worries, and distractions that keep our minds perpetually occupied. It is like having an endless list of browser tabs open in our brains, each one demanding attention, draining resources, and slowing us down. While some of this mental activity is inevitable, excessive mental clutter can become a serious impediment to living a peaceful and fulfilling life. Here's why:

1. **Lack of Focus and Clarity**

   Mental clutter scatters our attention, making it challenging to focus on the present moment. This lack of focus creates a sense of disorientation, where even simple tasks feel monumental, and clear decision-making becomes a struggle.

2. **Increased Stress and Anxiety**

   Cluttered minds are breeding grounds for stress and anxiety. Persistent worries and unresolved issues compete for attention, amplifying a sense of urgency and leaving us in a perpetual state of mental tension. This not only affects our emotional well-being but can also take a toll on our physical health.

3. **Emotional Overload**

   Unprocessed emotions add layers to mental clutter. Whether it's regret about the past, fear of the future, or resentment toward unresolved conflicts, these emotions linger in the background, influencing our thoughts and behaviors. Emotional overload can make it difficult to experience joy, gratitude, and connection.

4. **Disconnection from the Present**
Mental clutter often keeps us trapped in a cycle of rumination and overthinking. This fixation on what has happened or what might happen prevents us from engaging fully in the present moment, where peace and contentment naturally reside.

5. **Reduced Creativity and Problem-Solving**
A cluttered mind stifles creativity and hampers our ability to think critically or solve problems effectively. When our mental bandwidth is consumed by distractions and worries, we miss opportunities for innovation and insight.

6. **Energy Drain**
Just as a cluttered physical environment can feel exhausting, mental clutter drains our energy. The constant juggling of incomplete thoughts, to-do lists, and worries leaves little room for renewal, making us feel perpetually tired and burnt out.

The Importance of a Mental Reset

Recognizing the impact of mental clutter is the first step toward reclaiming our inner peace. A mental reset offers the opportunity to clear the noise, refocus our thoughts, and realign our priorities. This process is not merely about relaxation; it's about actively decluttering the mind, creating space for clarity, and fostering a state of balance and harmony.

1. **Rediscovering Peace**

   A mental reset allows us to silence the noise and reconnect with our inner selves. It provides the breathing room needed to process thoughts and emotions, cultivating a sense of calm and serenity.

2. **Enhanced Focus and Productivity**

   By clearing mental clutter, a reset sharpens our focus, enabling us to channel our energy toward meaningful tasks. It helps us break free from the paralysis of overthinking and take purposeful action.

3. **Emotional Healing**

   Taking time to reset mentally allows us to acknowledge and process lingering emotions. This healing process fosters emotional resilience, freeing us from the weight of unresolved issues.

4. **Living in the Present**

   A mental reset encourages mindfulness, the practice of fully experiencing the present moment. When we are grounded in the here and now, we can appreciate life's simple pleasures and respond to challenges with grace.

5. **Boosted Creativity and Problem-Solving**

   With mental clarity restored, our creative energies can flow more freely. A reset removes the fog of distraction, empowering us to approach problems with fresh perspectives and innovative solutions.

6. Recharging Energy Levels

Just as rest rejuvenates the body, a mental reset rejuvenates the mind. It allows us to conserve and redirect our energy, enabling us to face life's demands with renewed vigor.

Conclusion

Mental clutter may be a common byproduct of modern life, but it doesn't have to define our existence. By understanding its impact and committing to a mental reset, we can reclaim our peace, enhance our focus, and live more intentionally. This book will guide you through practical steps and transformative strategies to clear your mental clutter, reset your mind, and cultivate a life of clarity, purpose, and peace. Together, let us embark on this journey toward mental freedom and rediscover the joy of a decluttered mind.

Chapter 1: Clearing Mental Clutter

Our minds are our most powerful assets, yet they are often burdened with clutter that hinders peace, focus, and productivity. Mental clutter, much like physical clutter, can accumulate unnoticed over time, leaving us overwhelmed and emotionally drained. Clearing mental clutter is the first and most crucial step toward achieving mental clarity and a renewed sense of purpose. In this chapter, we'll explore how to identify emotional and mental stressors and implement simple yet effective steps to declutter your mind.

Identifying Emotional and Mental Stressors

Before we can begin decluttering our minds, it is essential to identify the sources of mental clutter. These stressors often stem from a variety of internal and external factors, and recognizing them is the first step toward managing and ultimately eliminating them.

1. **Unresolved Emotional Baggage**
    ◦ **Examples:** Regrets, guilt, resentment, grief, or anger.
    ◦ **Impact:** These emotions often linger in the background, draining mental energy and distorting our perception of the present.
    ◦ **Signs to Look For:** Persistent thoughts about past events, feelings of bitterness, or difficulty letting go of certain memories.
2. **Overcommitment and Unrealistic Expectations**
    ◦ **Examples:** Taking on too many responsibilities, saying "yes" when you mean "no," or setting unattainable goals.

- **Impact:** Overcommitment leads to stress, burnout, and a sense of failure when expectations aren't met.
- **Signs to Look For:** Constantly feeling behind schedule, dissatisfaction with achievements, or neglecting personal needs.

3. **Information Overload**
   - **Examples:** Endless social media scrolling, non-stop news updates, or an overreliance on digital devices.
   - **Impact:** The constant influx of information can overwhelm the brain, making it difficult to process or retain meaningful knowledge.
   - **Signs to Look For:** Difficulty focusing, feeling overstimulated, or an inability to "unplug."

4. **Negative Thought Patterns**
   - **Examples:** Self-doubt, catastrophizing, or overthinking.
   - **Impact:** These patterns create a feedback loop of negativity, reducing confidence and increasing anxiety.
   - **Signs to Look For:** Frequent self-criticism, fear of failure, or obsessing over worst-case scenarios.

5. **Unfinished Tasks and Unclear Priorities**
   - **Examples:** A cluttered to-do list, forgotten goals, or neglected responsibilities.
   - **Impact:** Open loops in our minds cause stress and a persistent sense of incompletion.
   - **Signs to Look For:** Feeling overwhelmed by tasks, procrastination, or anxiety about deadlines.

6. **Toxic Relationships and Environments**
   - **Examples:** People or situations that drain your energy, cause conflict, or perpetuate negativity.
   - **Impact:** Toxic relationships can consume mental space, leading to emotional exhaustion.

- ○ **Signs to Look For:** Feeling emotionally drained after interactions, dread about certain social engagements, or inability to establish boundaries.

By identifying these mental and emotional stressors, you can begin the process of decluttering your mind and regaining control over your mental space.

Simple Steps to Declutter Your Mind

Clearing mental clutter doesn't require a complete life overhaul. Small, deliberate actions taken consistently can have a profound impact. Below are practical steps you can take to declutter your mind and create space for peace and clarity.

1. **Practice Mindfulness**
   - **How:** Engage in mindfulness exercises like deep breathing, meditation, or yoga.
   - **Why:** Mindfulness helps anchor you to the present moment, reducing the influence of distracting thoughts.
   - **Tips:** Start with just five minutes a day of focused breathing or a guided meditation app.
2. **Journaling**
   - **How:** Write down your thoughts, worries, and goals in a journal.
   - **Why:** Journaling helps externalize your mental clutter, making it easier to process emotions and organize priorities.
   - **Tips:** Use prompts like, "What is weighing on my mind today?" or "What can I let go of?"
3. **Create a To-Do List**
   - **How:** List tasks in order of priority and break them into manageable steps.
   - **Why:** A clear plan reduces mental overwhelm by giving you a sense of control over your responsibilities.
   - **Tips:** Use the Eisenhower Matrix to classify tasks into urgent/important categories.
4. **Limit Information Consumption**
   - **How:** Set boundaries for screen time and information intake.

- **Why:** Reducing information overload creates mental space for focus and creativity.
- **Tips:** Schedule "tech-free" hours or designate a time for catching up on news or social media.

5. **Practice Emotional Release**
   - **How:** Acknowledge and process your emotions through therapy, talking to a trusted friend, or creative outlets like art or music.
   - **Why:** Letting go of suppressed emotions prevents them from turning into mental clutter.
   - **Tips:** Try techniques like writing an unsent letter or practicing gratitude to shift your emotional perspective.

6. **Declutter Your Physical Environment**
   - **How:** Organize your living and working spaces.
   - **Why:** Physical clutter often mirrors mental clutter; tidying up can lead to a clearer mind.
   - **Tips:** Start small, like cleaning one drawer or desk, and notice the immediate mental relief.

7. **Set Boundaries**
   - **How:** Learn to say no to unnecessary commitments and toxic interactions.
   - **Why:** Boundaries protect your time, energy, and mental space.
   - **Tips:** Use polite but firm language like, "I'm sorry, but I can't commit to that right now."

8. **Adopt a Minimalist Mindset**
   - **How:** Focus on what truly matters by eliminating distractions and unnecessary obligations.
   - **Why:** Simplifying your life reduces the sources of mental clutter.
   - **Tips:** Periodically review your schedule, relationships, and habits to identify what adds value versus what creates stress.

9. **Engage in Physical Activity**
    ◦ **How:** Incorporate regular exercise, such as walking, running, or stretching, into your routine.
    ◦ **Why:** Physical activity reduces stress hormones, boosts mood, and improves mental clarity.
    ◦ **Tips:** Even a 10-minute walk outdoors can have a calming effect.
10. **Develop a Nightly Brain Dump Routine**
    ◦ **How:** Spend a few minutes each evening writing down lingering thoughts or worries.
    ◦ **Why:** A brain dump clears your mind before sleep, allowing for more restful and restorative rest.
    ◦ **Tips:** Keep a notepad by your bed and jot down anything that comes to mind without overthinking.

Conclusion

Clearing mental clutter is a powerful practice that lays the foundation for greater peace, focus, and emotional well-being. By identifying the stressors that contribute to mental clutter and taking intentional steps to address them, you can reclaim your mental space and achieve a clearer, more balanced state of mind. Remember, mental decluttering is not a one-time event but an ongoing journey. With consistency and dedication, you'll find yourself more present, productive, and at peace.

Chapter 2: The 5-Minute Reset Ritual

In a world filled with constant distractions and demands, achieving calm and focus can often feel like an elusive goal. However, peace of mind doesn't require hours of meditation or a secluded retreat. With a simple 5-minute reset ritual, you can reclaim your mental clarity and restore balance throughout your day. This chapter will introduce daily practices for cultivating calm and focus and explore grounding and mindfulness techniques that can transform those fleeting moments of chaos into opportunities for renewal.

Daily Practices for Calm and Focus

The 5-minute reset ritual is designed to help you pause, center yourself, and return to a state of mental equilibrium. These daily practices, when consistently implemented, can create a ripple effect of peace and focus in every aspect of your life.

1. **Morning Intentions**
   - **What to Do:** Begin each day by setting a positive intention. Reflect on what you aim to accomplish or how you wish to feel throughout the day.
   - **Why It Works:** Starting your day with clarity helps you maintain focus and reduces unnecessary mental noise.
   - **Example Ritual:** Before checking your phone or diving into your to-do list, take a moment to say, "Today, I choose calm and clarity," or another affirmation that resonates with you.

2. **Breathing Breaks**
   - **What to Do:** Incorporate short, intentional breathing exercises into your day.
   - **Why It Works:** Deep breathing activates the parasympathetic nervous system, which calms the mind and body.
   - **Example Ritual:** Try the 4-4-4-4 method: inhale for 4 seconds, hold for 4 seconds, exhale for 4 seconds, and pause for 4 seconds before repeating.

3. **The Power of Gratitude**
  - **What to Do:** Spend a few moments reflecting on or writing down three things you are grateful for.
  - **Why It Works:** Gratitude shifts your focus from stressors to positive aspects of your life, promoting mental clarity and emotional balance.
  - **Example Ritual:** Keep a gratitude journal on your desk or nightstand and jot down a quick list each morning or evening.

4. **Mindful Transitions**
  - **What to Do:** Use transitions between activities as opportunities to reset.
  - **Why It Works:** Pausing between tasks creates space for mental renewal and reduces overwhelm.
  - **Example Ritual:** Before starting a new task, close your eyes, take three deep breaths, and consciously release any lingering tension.

5. **Evening Reflection**
  - **What to Do:** End your day with a brief reflection on what went well and what you can improve tomorrow.
  - **Why It Works:** This practice helps you process your day, let go of stress, and prepare your mind for restful sleep.
  - **Example Ritual:** Ask yourself, "What did I learn today?" or "What am I proud of?" to cultivate a sense of accomplishment and growth.

Techniques for Grounding and Mindfulness

Grounding and mindfulness techniques are essential components of the 5-minute reset ritual. These practices help anchor you to the present moment, reducing stress and improving focus.

1. **Grounding Through the Five Senses**
   - **What to Do:** Engage your senses to reconnect with the present moment.
   - **How:**
     - Identify **5 things you can see** around you.
     - Identify **4 things you can touch** and focus on their texture.
     - Identify **3 things you can hear**, like distant sounds or your own breath.
     - Identify **2 things you can smell**, or imagine pleasant scents.
     - Identify **1 thing you can taste**, like a sip of water or a mint.
   - **Why It Works:** This technique reduces anxiety by grounding your awareness in the physical world.
2. **Body Scan Meditation**
   - **What to Do:** Perform a quick mental scan of your body, noting any areas of tension or discomfort.
   - **How:**
     - Sit comfortably and close your eyes.
     - Start at the top of your head and slowly move your awareness down through your body, relaxing each part as you go.
   - **Why It Works:** This exercise promotes relaxation and increases awareness of physical and emotional states.

3. **Box Breathing for Mindfulness**
   - ◦ **What to Do:** Use controlled breathing to anchor your focus.
   - ◦ **How:**
     - Inhale for 4 seconds.
     - Hold your breath for 4 seconds.
     - Exhale for 4 seconds.
     - Hold your breath again for 4 seconds.
     - Repeat for 5 minutes.
   - ◦ **Why It Works:** Box breathing calms the nervous system and helps regulate emotional responses.

4. **Mindful Observation**
   - ◦ **What to Do:** Choose a simple object or element in your environment and observe it closely.
   - ◦ **How:**
     - Look at a flower, a candle flame, or even a cup of tea.
     - Pay attention to its colors, shapes, textures, and movements.
   - ◦ **Why It Works:** Mindful observation trains your mind to focus on the present, quieting distractions.

5. **Grounding Through Movement**
   - ◦ **What to Do:** Engage in gentle physical activity like stretching, walking, or yoga.
   - ◦ **How:**
     - Pay attention to the sensations in your body as you move.
     - Synchronize your movements with your breath.
   - ◦ **Why It Works:** Movement helps release physical tension and brings your focus back to the body.

Creating Your Personalized 5-Minute Reset Ritual

The beauty of the 5-minute reset ritual is its adaptability. Here's how you can design a routine that works best for your lifestyle and needs:

1. **Identify Your Goal**
   - Decide what you want to achieve with your reset: relaxation, focus, or emotional balance.
2. **Choose Your Techniques**
   - Combine two or three techniques that resonate with you, such as box breathing, mindful observation, and gratitude.
3. **Set a Timer**
   - Allocate a dedicated 5 minutes for your ritual and use a timer to prevent distractions.
4. **Incorporate It Into Your Routine**
   - Schedule your reset at consistent times, such as in the morning, during a lunch break, or before bed.
5. **Track Your Progress**
   - Reflect on how your ritual impacts your mood, focus, and overall mental clarity. Adjust as needed.

Conclusion

The 5-minute reset ritual is a powerful tool for reclaiming calm and focus in a busy world. By incorporating daily practices and grounding techniques into your routine, you can create moments of peace that ripple throughout your day. Remember, the key to success lies in consistency and intentionality. Even in the midst of chaos, you can find clarity and balance in just five minutes. Let this ritual become your anchor, grounding you in the present and empowering you to navigate life with greater ease and confidence.

Chapter 3: Reframing Negativity

Negativity is an unavoidable aspect of life. We encounter challenges, setbacks, and difficulties that can feel overwhelming, leaving us trapped in a cycle of frustration and despair. However, the way we perceive and respond to these experiences can profoundly shape our lives. By reframing negativity, we can transform challenges into opportunities for growth and build emotional resilience to navigate life's ups and downs. This chapter explores how to shift perspectives, embrace adversity, and cultivate the strength to thrive in the face of hardship.

Turning Challenges into Growth Opportunities

Challenges, though often unwelcome, are catalysts for growth. They push us out of our comfort zones, teach us valuable lessons, and shape us into more capable individuals. Reframing negativity involves changing the way we interpret difficulties, seeing them not as roadblocks but as stepping stones toward personal development.

1. **The Power of Perspective**
   - **What It Means:** How we view a situation determines our emotional response to it. Viewing a setback as an insurmountable failure amplifies negativity, while seeing it as a learning experience fosters growth.
   - **How to Reframe:**
     - Ask yourself, "What can I learn from this situation?"
     - Consider how the challenge might benefit you in the long run.
     - Replace "Why is this happening to me?" with "What is this teaching me?"

2. **Embrace the Growth Mindset**
   - **Definition:** A growth mindset is the belief that abilities and intelligence can be developed through effort and learning.
   - **Why It Matters:** People with a growth mindset view challenges as opportunities to improve rather than as threats to their competence.
   - **How to Practice:**
     - Recognize that setbacks are temporary and part of the journey.
     - Celebrate progress, no matter how small, and view mistakes as stepping stones to success.

3. **Reframe Failure as Feedback**
   - **What It Means:** Failure is not a reflection of your worth but a form of feedback that provides clarity on what doesn't work.
   - **How to Reframe:**
     - List the lessons learned from a past failure and how they helped you grow.
     - Shift your language: Instead of saying, "I failed," say, "I discovered another way that doesn't work."

4. **Focus on What You Can Control**
   - **Why It Matters:** Dwelling on aspects of a challenge that you cannot change leads to helplessness. Shifting your focus to what you can influence fosters empowerment.
   - **How to Practice:**
     - Identify actionable steps to address the problem.
     - Use the Serenity Prayer approach: Accept what you cannot change, courageously change what you can, and seek the wisdom to know the difference.

5. **Visualize the Bigger Picture**
   - **Why It Matters:** In the midst of difficulty, it's easy to lose sight of the larger narrative of your life.

- **How to Practice:**
  - Ask, "How will I look back on this situation a year from now?"
  - Reflect on past challenges you've overcome and how they shaped your current strengths.

Building Emotional Resilience

Emotional resilience is the ability to bounce back from adversity, adapt to difficult situations, and maintain a sense of well-being. It doesn't mean avoiding negativity but rather developing the tools to navigate it effectively. Building resilience is a lifelong practice, and it starts with small, intentional steps.

1. **Recognize and Regulate Emotions**
   - **What It Means:** Emotional awareness is the foundation of resilience. Being attuned to your feelings helps you manage them constructively.
   - **How to Practice:**
     - Label your emotions when they arise: "I'm feeling frustrated," or "I'm feeling anxious."
     - Use grounding techniques, such as deep breathing or mindfulness, to regulate strong emotions.
2. **Cultivate Self-Compassion**
   - **Definition:** Self-compassion is treating yourself with kindness and understanding, especially during times of failure or struggle.
   - **Why It Matters:** Harsh self-criticism undermines resilience, while self-compassion fosters a supportive inner dialogue.
   - **How to Practice:**
     - Speak to yourself as you would to a friend. Replace "I'm so bad at this" with "I'm learning and improving."
     - Practice affirmations such as, "I am doing the best I can with what I have right now."

3. **Develop Healthy Coping Mechanisms**
    - **Why It Matters:** Resilience requires constructive ways to deal with stress and adversity.
    - **How to Practice:**
        - Engage in activities that bring you joy and relaxation, such as exercise, journaling, or creative hobbies.
        - Avoid unhealthy coping mechanisms, such as excessive screen time or substance use, which can amplify negativity.

4. **Strengthen Your Support System**
    - **Why It Matters:** Connection with others provides emotional support and perspective during challenging times.
    - **How to Practice:**
        - Reach out to trusted friends or family members when you need to talk.
        - Join a community or group that aligns with your interests or values.

5. **Practice Gratitude**
    - **What It Means:** Gratitude shifts your focus from what's wrong to what's right in your life.
    - **How to Practice:**
        - Keep a gratitude journal and write down three things you're thankful for each day.
        - Share your gratitude with others by expressing appreciation for their kindness or support.

6. **Develop Mental Flexibility**
    - **Definition:** Mental flexibility is the ability to adapt your thoughts and behaviors to new situations.
    - **Why It Matters:** Rigid thinking amplifies negativity, while flexibility helps you adjust to change more effectively.
    - **How to Practice:**

- Challenge automatic negative thoughts with alternative perspectives.
- Stay open to new solutions or approaches to problems.

7. **Focus on Purpose and Meaning**
   - **Why It Matters:** Having a sense of purpose provides motivation and perspective during adversity.
   - **How to Practice:**
     - Reflect on your values and what matters most to you.
     - Pursue activities or goals that align with your sense of purpose.

Practical Exercises for Reframing and Resilience

1. **The Negativity Flip**
   - **What to Do:** Write down a negative thought or situation and brainstorm at least three potential positive outcomes or lessons from it.
   - **Example:**
     - Negative: "I didn't get the promotion I wanted."
     - Positive Reframe: "I have more time to develop my skills and prepare for future opportunities."
2. **The Resilience Ladder**
   - **What to Do:** Break a large challenge into smaller, manageable steps and focus on completing them one at a time.
   - **Example:** If you're overwhelmed by financial stress, start by creating a budget, then explore additional income sources, and finally, set achievable savings goals.
3. **The Gratitude Reboot**
   - **What to Do:** When faced with a negative experience, identify at least one thing you are grateful for in the situation.
   - **Example:**
     - Challenge: "My car broke down."
     - Gratitude: "I'm thankful I have friends who can give me a ride or help me figure out repairs."

Conclusion

Reframing negativity and building emotional resilience are transformative practices that empower you to face life's challenges with grace and strength. By shifting your perspective and developing tools to manage adversity, you can unlock personal growth and cultivate a deeper sense of inner peace. Remember, negativity is not the enemy—it's an opportunity to grow, learn, and thrive. Let each challenge you face become a stepping stone toward the resilient, empowered version of yourself you're striving to be.

Chapter 4: Creating a Mental Sanctuary

In the whirlwind of daily life, having a mental sanctuary—a space within your mind and environment where peace and calmness reside—is essential for emotional and psychological well-being. A mental sanctuary serves as a retreat from stress, a haven where you can recharge and find clarity. This chapter will guide you in designing a space for inner peace and teach you rituals to reinforce calmness, helping you cultivate a sense of tranquility that you can carry with you anywhere.

How to Design a Space for Inner Peace

Designing a mental sanctuary begins with creating a physical environment that promotes relaxation and safety. Your external surroundings significantly influence your mental state, so crafting a peaceful physical space is the first step toward nurturing inner calm.

1. **Choose Your Sanctuary Space**
   - **What to Do:** Select a specific location in your home or workplace that will serve as your sanctuary.
   - **Characteristics to Look For:**
     - Quiet and free from distractions.
     - Comfortable and easy to access.
     - Personal, where you feel safe and relaxed.
   - **Examples:** A corner of your bedroom, a cozy chair by a window, or even a small garden.
2. **Declutter and Simplify**
   - **Why It Matters:** Physical clutter can create mental chaos. A clean, organized space fosters clarity and relaxation.
   - **How to Simplify:**

- Remove unnecessary items from your sanctuary space.
- Incorporate minimalistic décor to reduce visual distractions.
- Keep only items that bring you peace or joy.

3. **Incorporate Soothing Elements**
   - **What to Include:** Add elements to your space that evoke calmness and comfort.
   - **Ideas:**
     - **Lighting:** Use soft, warm lighting like candles, fairy lights, or lamps with dimmers.
     - **Textures:** Include cozy blankets, cushions, or rugs.
     - **Nature:** Add plants, flowers, or a small water feature like a tabletop fountain.
     - **Aromatherapy:** Use essential oils, incense, or scented candles with calming scents like lavender, sandalwood, or chamomile.

4. **Personalize Your Sanctuary**
   - **Why It Matters:** Personal touches make the space uniquely yours, fostering a deeper connection to your sanctuary.
   - **Ideas:**
     - Display meaningful objects like photos, mementos, or spiritual symbols.
     - Include a vision board, affirmations, or inspiring quotes.
     - Keep a journal or sketchpad for reflection and creativity.

5. **Create a Boundary**
   - **What It Means:** Define the purpose of your sanctuary and set boundaries to protect its peace.
   - **How to Protect Your Space:**

- Use it only for relaxation, reflection, or mindfulness practices.
- Inform others in your household that this space is your retreat and ask for uninterrupted time when you're using it.

Rituals to Reinforce Calmness

Once your sanctuary is designed, rituals can help anchor its purpose and create a sense of calm that transcends the physical space. Rituals are intentional practices that signal to your mind and body that it's time to relax, reflect, or reset.

1. **Morning Grounding Ritual**
   - **What to Do:** Begin your day with a grounding practice in your sanctuary.
   - **How:**
     - Sit comfortably and take three deep breaths.
     - Visualize yourself rooted like a tree, strong and steady.
     - Set a positive intention for the day, such as "I will approach today with calm and clarity."
   - **Why It Works:** Starting your day in a state of mindfulness sets the tone for a peaceful and focused mindset.
2. **Meditation or Mindfulness Practice**
   - **What to Do:** Dedicate a few minutes daily to meditation or mindfulness in your sanctuary.
   - **How:**
     - Close your eyes and focus on your breath, observing it without judgment.
     - If your mind wanders, gently guide it back to your breath or a calming mantra.
   - **Why It Works:** Meditation helps quiet the mental noise and reinforces your sanctuary as a place of peace.

3. **Evening Wind-Down Ritual**
    - **What to Do:** Use your sanctuary to transition from the busyness of the day to a state of rest.
    - **How:**
        - Light a candle or use a diffuser with calming essential oils.
        - Reflect on your day by journaling or practicing gratitude.
        - Perform a body scan meditation to release physical and emotional tension.
    - **Why It Works:** An evening ritual signals your brain to let go of the day's stress and prepare for restful sleep.
4. **Visualization Practice**
    - **What to Do:** Use your sanctuary for visualization exercises that transport you to a serene mental space.
    - **How:**
        - Close your eyes and imagine yourself in a calming environment, such as a beach, forest, or meadow.
        - Engage all your senses: feel the sand beneath your feet, hear the rustle of leaves, and smell the fresh air.
    - **Why It Works:** Visualization helps create a mental sanctuary you can access anytime, even outside your physical retreat.
5. **Sound Therapy**
    - **What to Do:** Incorporate soothing sounds into your sanctuary rituals.
    - **How:**
        - Play calming music, nature sounds, or white noise.
        - Use a singing bowl or tuning fork for vibrational healing.
    - **Why It Works:** Sound therapy reduces stress and enhances relaxation.

6.Creative Expression

- **What to Do:** Use your sanctuary as a space for creative expression, such as drawing, writing, or playing music.
- **How:**
    - Dedicate time to a creative activity that brings you joy.
    - Focus on the process rather than the outcome.
- **Why It Works:** Creativity is a powerful outlet for stress and fosters a sense of flow and fulfillment.
-
- ### 7.Affirmation Ritual
    - **What to Do:** Use positive affirmations to cultivate a calm and empowered mindset.
    - **How:**
        - Write or say affirmations aloud, such as "I am at peace," or "My mind is calm and clear."
        - Repeat them daily in your sanctuary.
    - **Why It Works:** Affirmations rewire your brain to focus on positivity and resilience.
    -
    - ### 8.Periodic Sanctuary Reset
        - **What to Do:** Regularly refresh your sanctuary to keep it aligned with your needs.
        - **How:**
            - Rearrange items, add new elements, or clean and declutter the space.
        - **Why It Works:** A periodic reset reinvigorates the energy of your sanctuary and keeps it a source of inspiration.

Benefits of a Mental Sanctuary

Creating and maintaining a mental sanctuary provides numerous benefits that ripple into every aspect of your life:

1. **Enhanced Stress Management**
   - A dedicated space for relaxation helps you manage stress more effectively.
2. **Improved Focus and Productivity**
   - Regular use of your sanctuary can improve mental clarity, enhancing your ability to focus.
3. **Stronger Emotional Regulation**
   - Sanctuary rituals provide tools for processing emotions, fostering emotional resilience.
4. **Deeper Connection to Self**
   - Spending intentional time in your sanctuary strengthens self-awareness and inner peace.
5. **Portable Calmness**
   - Practicing rituals in your sanctuary builds habits that can be replicated anywhere, helping you stay calm even in stressful environments.

Conclusion

Creating a mental sanctuary is a transformative act of self-care. By designing a physical space for inner peace and incorporating rituals that nurture calmness, you establish a foundation for mental and emotional well-being. Your sanctuary becomes a sacred space where you can recharge, reflect, and reconnect with yourself. Over time, the tranquility cultivated in this space will extend beyond its walls, empowering you to carry a sense of peace with you wherever you go. Let this sanctuary be your refuge, a place where calm and clarity are always within reach.

Chapter 5: A Lifetime of Mental Clarity

Achieving mental clarity is not a one-time event but a lifelong journey. It requires the consistent practice of habits that promote peace, focus, and emotional balance. In a world filled with unexpected challenges and persistent distractions, maintaining these habits and managing stress over the long term ensures you can navigate life with resilience and confidence. This chapter explores strategies for cultivating mental clarity as a sustainable practice, helping you manage stress and chaos for the long haul.

Maintaining the Habits of a Clear Mind

Developing mental clarity begins with intentional habits. Sustaining this clarity over a lifetime requires a commitment to those habits, even as life evolves. By integrating these practices into your daily routine, you can create a foundation for enduring peace and focus.

1. **Commit to Daily Reflection**
   - **Why It Matters:** Regular self-reflection helps you stay aligned with your goals and identify areas of mental clutter.
   - **How to Practice:**
     - Dedicate 5–10 minutes daily to journaling your thoughts, reviewing your day, and setting intentions for tomorrow.
     - Ask yourself reflective questions like, "What did I accomplish today?" or "What thoughts are no longer serving me?"
2. **Stay Mindful in the Present Moment**
   - **Why It Matters:** Mindfulness anchors you to the present, reducing overthinking and worry about the past or future.
   - **How to Practice:**

- Incorporate mindfulness techniques like deep breathing, body scans, or focused attention on daily activities.
- Use reminders, such as a gentle alarm or a visual cue, to bring your focus back to the moment when your mind wanders.

3. **Adopt a Growth Mindset**
   - **Why It Matters:** A growth mindset fosters adaptability, allowing you to embrace challenges as opportunities for improvement.
   - **How to Practice:**
     - Reframe setbacks as learning experiences.
     - Regularly challenge yourself with new skills or projects that promote growth and self-improvement.

4. **Prioritize Your Physical Health**
   - **Why It Matters:** A healthy body supports a clear mind. Poor physical health, such as lack of sleep or a sedentary lifestyle, can contribute to mental fog.
   - **How to Practice:**
     - Prioritize sleep, aiming for 7–9 hours each night.
     - Engage in regular physical activity, such as walking, yoga, or strength training.
     - Maintain a balanced diet with brain-boosting foods like leafy greens, nuts, and omega-3-rich fish.

5. **Simplify and Declutter Regularly**
   - **Why It Matters:** Both physical and mental clutter can accumulate over time, disrupting clarity and focus.
   - **How to Practice:**
     - Periodically declutter your environment, removing items you no longer need.
     - Perform mental decluttering by revisiting goals and eliminating tasks or commitments that no longer align with your priorities.

6. **Nurture Meaningful Connections**
    - ◦ **Why It Matters:** Supportive relationships foster emotional well-being and provide perspective during challenging times.
    - ◦ **How to Practice:**
        - ▪ Schedule regular time to connect with friends, family, or mentors.
        - ▪ Foster deeper connections by being present, listening actively, and sharing your thoughts and feelings.

Managing Stress and Chaos Long-Term

Life is inherently unpredictable, and no one is immune to stress or chaos. However, with the right strategies, you can build resilience and maintain mental clarity even in the face of life's challenges. Here are practices to help you manage stress and chaos over the long term.

1. **Develop a Resilience Toolbox**
    - **What It Is:** A collection of strategies and practices you can rely on during stressful times.
    - **How to Build It:**
        - Include quick resets like breathing exercises, mindfulness techniques, and grounding practices.
        - Identify longer-term tools, such as therapy, creative outlets, or support groups, to help you navigate more significant challenges.
2. **Establish Flexible Routines**
    - **Why It Matters:** Consistent routines provide structure, but flexibility allows you to adapt when circumstances change.
    - **How to Practice:**
        - Create morning and evening routines that include time for reflection, mindfulness, and self-care.
        - Allow room in your schedule for unexpected changes without sacrificing your core habits.
3. **Set Healthy Boundaries**
    - **Why It Matters:** Protecting your time and energy is essential for preventing burnout and maintaining focus.
    - **How to Practice:**

- Learn to say no to commitments that do not align with your priorities.
- Establish limits with work, relationships, or technology to prevent overextension.

4. **Practice Emotional Regulation**
   - **Why It Matters:** Strong emotions can cloud judgment and exacerbate stress. Learning to manage them effectively is key to mental clarity.
   - **How to Practice:**
     - Identify your emotional triggers and develop constructive ways to respond.
     - Use techniques like journaling, deep breathing, or talking to a trusted friend to process emotions healthily.

5. **Focus on What You Can Control**
   - **Why It Matters:** Dwelling on uncontrollable factors leads to frustration and anxiety, while focusing on actionable steps fosters empowerment.
   - **How to Practice:**
     - When faced with stress, ask yourself, "What is within my control?"
     - Direct your energy toward those actions, whether it's creating a plan, seeking support, or adjusting your perspective.

6. **Recharge Through Rest and Play**
   - **Why It Matters:** Chronic stress depletes your mental and emotional reserves. Regular rest and play help restore balance and clarity.
   - **How to Practice:**
     - Schedule downtime for relaxation and hobbies that bring you joy.
     - Avoid guilt about rest, recognizing it as essential for long-term productivity and well-being.

7. **Reassess and Realign Regularly**
    - **Why It Matters:** Life evolves, and so do your needs and priorities. Periodic reassessment ensures your habits and goals remain aligned with your current reality.
    - **How to Practice:**
        - Every few months, review your goals, routines, and mental state.
        - Make adjustments as needed to reflect changes in your life or circumstances.

8. **Invest in Self-Development**
    - **Why It Matters:** Personal growth fosters resilience and clarity, helping you handle stress and chaos with greater confidence.
    - **How to Practice:**
        - Engage in activities that promote learning and growth, such as reading, taking courses, or attending workshops.
        - Reflect on how these experiences enhance your ability to navigate challenges.

Practical Exercises for Long-Term Clarity

1. **The Weekly Clarity Check-In**
    - **What to Do:** Set aside time each week to evaluate your mental state and habits.
    - **How:**
        - Reflect on what worked well during the week and what caused stress.
        - Adjust your schedule or habits based on these reflections.
2. **Stress Journaling**
    - **What to Do:** When overwhelmed, write down your stressors and categorize them into what you can and cannot control.
    - **How It Helps:** This exercise helps you prioritize actionable steps and release worries about uncontrollable factors.
3. **Visualization for Long-Term Goals**
    - **What to Do:** Regularly visualize your ideal future self, focusing on clarity, peace, and resilience.
    - **How It Helps:** Visualization reinforces your commitment to mental clarity and helps you stay motivated during challenging times.

Conclusion

A lifetime of mental clarity requires intentional effort, adaptability, and a commitment to self-care. By maintaining habits that promote a clear mind and adopting strategies to manage stress and chaos, you can create a resilient foundation for navigating life's uncertainties. Mental clarity is not about achieving perfection but about cultivating a state of balance and focus that allows you to handle whatever comes your way with confidence and grace. Let these practices become your lifelong companions, guiding you toward a life filled with purpose, peace, and enduring clarity.

Appendix A: Guided Journaling Prompts for Clarity

Journaling is one of the most effective tools for achieving and maintaining mental clarity. It provides a safe space to explore your thoughts, process emotions, and reflect on your priorities. This appendix offers a collection of guided journaling prompts specifically designed to help you clear your mind, gain insight, and cultivate inner peace. Use these prompts regularly to unlock new perspectives, overcome mental clutter, and reconnect with your purpose.

Section 1: Morning Clarity Prompts

These prompts are designed to help you start your day with focus and intention. Spend 5–10 minutes on one or more of these prompts each morning to set the tone for a productive and peaceful day.

1. **Setting Intentions**
   - What is my main focus for today?
   - How do I want to feel throughout the day?
   - What one thing can I do today to bring myself closer to my goals?

2. **Gratitude and Positivity**
   - What are three things I am grateful for this morning?
   - What excites me about today?
   - What positive thought or affirmation will guide me today?

3. **Identifying Priorities**
   - What are the top three tasks I need to complete today?
   - What is one thing I can let go of to reduce stress?
   - Where can I create more time or space for myself today?

Section 2: Evening Reflection Prompts

Use these prompts at the end of your day to reflect on your experiences, process emotions, and prepare your mind for restful sleep. Evening journaling is an excellent way to clear mental clutter and let go of any unresolved tension.

1. **Daily Wins and Gratitude**
   - What went well today, and why?
   - What is one thing I am proud of from today?
   - What small moments brought me joy or peace today?
2. **Lessons and Growth**
   - What challenges did I face today, and what did I learn from them?
   - How did I grow or improve today?
   - What is one thing I would do differently tomorrow?
3. **Letting Go**
   - What thoughts or worries am I ready to release before bed?
   - Is there anything unresolved from today that I can address tomorrow?
   - How can I show myself kindness and compassion tonight?

Section 3: Weekly Clarity Prompts

At the end of each week, use these prompts to evaluate your progress, celebrate your successes, and reset your intentions for the week ahead. Weekly reflection helps you maintain a clear sense of direction and adapt to any changes.

1. **Reflection on the Week**
   - What were the highlights of my week?
   - What challenges did I face, and how did I handle them?
   - What did I learn about myself this week?

2. **Evaluating Goals and Priorities**
   - Did I achieve what I set out to do this week? Why or why not?
   - What is one goal I want to carry into next week?
   - Are there any commitments or habits I need to adjust to align better with my priorities?

3. **Self-Care and Balance**
   - How well did I take care of myself this week?
   - What activities or practices helped me feel balanced and centered?
   - What can I do next week to nurture my mental and emotional well-being?

Section 4: Overcoming Mental Clutter

When you feel overwhelmed or mentally cluttered, these prompts can help you identify and clear the sources of your stress. Use them whenever you need a mental reset.

1. **Identifying Clutter**
    ◦ What thoughts or worries are currently weighing on my mind?
    ◦ Are there any unfinished tasks or unresolved issues creating mental tension?
    ◦ What fears or doubts are holding me back right now?

2. **Clearing the Clutter**
    ◦ What steps can I take to resolve or let go of these worries?
    ◦ What is one small action I can take today to reduce stress?
    ◦ Who or what can I turn to for support?

3. **Reframing Challenges**
    ◦ How can I view this situation as an opportunity for growth?
    ◦ What lessons or insights can I gain from this experience?
    ◦ How would my future self advise me to handle this?

Section 5: Cultivating Gratitude and Positivity

Gratitude journaling is a powerful way to shift your focus from negativity to positivity. These prompts are designed to help you cultivate an attitude of gratitude and strengthen your emotional resilience.

1. **Daily Gratitude**
   - What are three things I am grateful for today, and why?
   - Who in my life am I thankful for, and how can I show them appreciation?
   - What simple pleasures brought me happiness today?
2. **Finding the Silver Lining**
   - What is one positive thing that came out of a recent challenge?
   - What unexpected blessing or opportunity have I experienced lately?
   - How can I use gratitude to reframe a difficult situation?
3. **Gratitude for Self**
   - What personal strength or quality am I grateful for?
   - What is one way I have grown or improved recently?
   - How can I celebrate and honor myself today?

Section 6: Vision and Goal Setting

Journaling about your vision and goals helps you stay focused on your aspirations and align your daily actions with your long-term purpose. Use these prompts to clarify your direction and maintain motivation.

1. **Clarifying Your Vision**
   - What does my ideal life look and feel like?
   - What are my core values, and how do they shape my goals?
   - What legacy do I want to leave behind?

2. **Setting Goals**
   - What are three goals I want to achieve this month?
   - What specific steps can I take to move closer to these goals?
   - How will achieving these goals improve my life?

3. **Tracking Progress**
   - What progress have I made toward my goals, and what have I learned along the way?
   - What obstacles have I encountered, and how can I overcome them?
   - How can I stay motivated and focused on my vision?

Section 7: Emotional Clarity and Healing

Emotional clarity is essential for mental peace. These prompts are designed to help you process emotions, resolve conflicts, and cultivate inner healing.

1. **Processing Emotions**
   - What emotion am I feeling most strongly right now, and why?
   - How can I express or release this emotion constructively?
   - What does this emotion teach me about my needs or desires?
2. **Healing from the Past**
   - What past experience or memory still affects me today?
   - What steps can I take to heal or move forward from this experience?
   - How can I practice forgiveness—toward myself or others?
3. **Nurturing Self-Compassion**
   - What do I need most from myself right now?
   - How can I show myself kindness and understanding in this moment?
   - What affirmation or mantra can I repeat to soothe my mind and heart?

Conclusion

These guided journaling prompts are tools for reflection, growth, and clarity. Whether you use them daily, weekly, or during moments of mental clutter, they can help you explore your thoughts, identify solutions, and cultivate a deeper connection with yourself. Keep this appendix as a resource to guide your journaling practice and support your journey toward a lifetime of mental clarity and peace.

<u>Message from the Author:</u>

I hope you enjoyed this book, I love astrology and knew there was not a book such as this out on the shelf. I love metaphysical items as well. Please check out my other books:

-Life of Government Benefits

-My life of Hell

-My life with Hydrocephalus

-Red Sky

-World Domination:Woman's rule

-World Domination:Woman's Rule 2: The War

-Life and Banishment of Apophis: book 1

-The Kidney Friendly Diet

-The Ultimate Hemp Cookbook

-Creating a Dispensary(legally)

-Cleanliness throughout life: the importance of showering from childhood to adulthood.

-Strong Roots: The Risks of Overcoddling children

-Hemp Horoscopes: Cosmic Insights and Earthly Healing

- Celestial Hemp Navigating the Zodiac: Through the Green Cosmos

-Astrological Hemp: Aligning The Stars with Earth's Ancient Herb

-The Astrological Guide to Hemp: Stars, Signs, and Sacred Leaves

-Green Growth: Innovative Marketing Strategies for your Hemp Products and Dispensary

-Cosmic Cannabis

-Astrological Munchies

-Henry The Hemp

-Zodiacal Roots: The Astrological Soul Of Hemp

- Green Constellations: Intersection of Hemp and Zodiac

-Hemp in The Houses: An astrological Adventure Through The Cannabis Galaxy

-Galactic Ganja Guide

Heavenly Hemp

Zodiac Leaves

Doctor Who Astrology

Cannastrology

Stellar Satvias and Cosmic Indicas

Celestial Cannabis: A Zodiac Journey

AstroHerbology: The Sky and The Soil: Volume 1

AstroHerbology:Celestial Cannabis:Volume 2

Cosmic Cannabis Cultivation

The Starry Guide to Herbal Harmony: Volume 1

The Starry Guide to Herbal Harmony: Cannabis Universe: Volume 2

Yugioh Astrology: Astrological Guide to Deck, Duels and more

Nightmare Mansion: Echoes of The Abyss

Nightmare Mansion 2: Legacy of Shadows

Nightmare Mansion 3: Shadows of the Forgotten

Nightmare Mansion 4: Echoes of the Damned

The Life and Banishment of Apophis: Book 2

Nightmare Mansion: Halls of Despair

Healing with Herb: Cannabis and Hydrocephalus

Planetary Pot: Aligning with Astrological Herbs: Volume 1

Fast Track to Freedom: 30 Days to Financial Independence Using AI, Assets, and Agile Hustles

Cosmic Hemp Pathways

How to Become Financially Free in 30 Days: 10,000 Paths to Prosperity

Zodiacal Herbage: Astrological Insights: Volume 1

Nightmare Mansion: Whispers in the Walls

The Daleks Invade Atlantis
Henry the hemp and Hydrocephalus

10X The Kidney Friendly Diet
Cannabis Universe: Adult coloring book
Hemp Astrology: The Healing Power of the Stars
Zodiacal Herbage: Astrological Insights: Cannabis Universe: Volume 2
<u>Planetary Pot: Aligning with Astrological Herbs: Cannabis Universes: Volume 2</u>
Doctor Who Meets the Replicators and SG-1: The Ultimate Battle for Survival
Nightmare Mansion: Curse of the Blood Moon
<u>The Celestial Stoner: A Guide to the Zodiac</u>
Cosmic Pleasures: Sex Toy Astrology for Every Sign
Hydrocephalus Astrology: Navigating the Stars and Healing Waters
Lapis and the Mischievous Chocolate Bar

Celestial Positions: Sexual Astrology for Every Sign
Apophis's Shadow Work Journal: **:** A Journey of Self-Discovery and Healing
Kinky Cosmos: Sexual Kink Astrology for Every Sign
Digital Cosmos: The Astrological Digimon Compendium
Stellar Seeds: The Cosmic Guide to Growing with Astrology
Apophis's Daily Gratitude Journal

Cat Astrology: Feline Mysteries of the Cosmos
The Cosmic Kama Sutra: An Astrological Guide to Sexual Positions
Unleash Your Potential: A Guided Journal Powered by AI Insights
Whispers of the Enchanted Grove

Cosmic Pleasures: An Astrological Guide to Sexual Kinks

369, 12 Manifestation Journal

Whisper of the nocturne journal(blank journal for writing or drawing)

The Boogey Book

Locked In Reflection: A Chastity Journey Through Locktober

Generating Wealth Quickly:

How to Generate $100,000 in 24 Hours

Star Magic: Harness the Power of the Universe

The Flatulence Chronicles: A Fart Journal for Self-Discovery

The Doctor and The Death Moth

Seize the Day: A Personal Seizure Tracking Journal

The Ultimate Boogeyman Safari: A Journey into the Boogie World and Beyond

Whispers of Samhain: 1,000 Spells of Love, Luck, and Lunar Magic: Samhain Spell Book

Apophis's guides:

Witch's Spellbook Crafting Guide for Halloween

<u>Frost & Flame: The Enchanted Yule Grimoire of 1000 Winter Spells</u>

<u>The Ultimate Boogey Goo Guide & Spooky Activities for Halloween Fun</u>

Harmony of the Scales: A Libra's Spellcraft for Balance and Beauty

The Enchanted Advent: 36 Days of Christmas Wonders

Nightmare Mansion: The Labyrinth of Screams

Harvest of Enchantment: 1,000 Spells of Gratitude, Love, and Fortune for Thanksgiving

The Boogey Chronicles: A Journal of Nightly Encounters and Shadowy Secrets

The 12 Days of Financial Freedom: A Step-by-Step Christmas Countdown to Transform Your Finances

Sigil of the Eternal Spiral Blank Journal

A Christmas Feast: Timeless Recipes for Every Meal

Holiday Stress-Free Solutions: A Survival Guide to Thriving During the Festive Season

Yu-Gi-Oh! Holiday Gifting Mastery: The Ultimate Guide for Fans and Newcomers Alike

Holiday Harmony: A Hydrocephalus Survival Guide for the Festive Season

Celestial Craft: The Witch's Almanac for 2025 – A Cosmic Guide to Manifestations, Moons, and Mystical Events

Doctor Who: The Toymaker's Winter Wonderland

Tulsa King Unveiled: A Thrilling Guide to Stallone's Mafia Masterpiece

Pendulum Craft: A Complete Guide to Crafting and Using Personalized Divination Tools

Nightmare Mansion: Santa's Eternal Eve

Starlight Noel: A Cosmic Journey through Christmas Mysteries

The Dark Architect: Unlocking the Blueprint of Existence

Surviving the Embrace: The Ultimate Guide to Encounters with The Hugging Molly

The Enchanted Codex: Secrets of the Craft for Witches, Wiccans, and Pagans

Harvest of Gratitude: A Complete Thanksgiving Guide

Yuletide Essentials: A Complete Guide to an Authentic and Magical Christmas

Celestial Smokes: A Cosmic Guide to Cigars and Astrology

Living in Balance: A Comprehensive Survival Guide to Thriving with Diabetes Insipidus

Cosmic Symbiosis: The Venom Zodiac Chronicles

The Cursed Paw of Ambition

Cosmic Symbiosis: The Astrological Venom Journal

Celestial Wonders Unfold: A Stargazer's Guide to the Cosmos (2024-2029)

The Ultimate Black Friday Prepper's Guide: Mastering Shopping Strategies and Savings

Cosmic Sales: The Astrological Guide to Black Friday Shopping

Legends of the Corn Mother and Other Harvest Myths

Whispers of the Harvest: The Corn Mother's Journal

The Evergreen Spellbook

The Doctor Meets the Boogeyman

The White Witch of Rose Hall's SpellBook

The Gingerbread Golem's Shadow: A Study in Sweet Darkness

The Gingerbread Golem Codex: An Academic Exploration of Sweet Myths

The Gingerbread Golem Grimoire: Sweet Magicks and Spells for the Festive Witch

The Curse of the Gingerbread Golem

10-minute Christmas Crafts for kids

<u>Christmas Crisis Solutions: The Ultimate Last-Minute Survival Guide</u>

Gingerbread Golem Recipes: Holiday Treats with a Magical Twist

The Infinite Key: Unlocking Mystical Secrets of the Ages

Enchanted Yule: A Wiccan and Pagan Guide to a Magical and Memorable Season

Dinosaurs of Power: Unlocking Ancient Magick

Astro-Dinos: The Cosmic Guide to Prehistoric Wisdom

Gallifrey's Yule Logs: A Festive Doctor Who Cookbook

The Dino Grimoire: Secrets of Prehistoric Magick

The Gift They Never Knew They Needed

The Gingerbread Golem's Culinary Alchemy: Enchanting Recipes for a Sweetly Dark Feast

A Time Lord Christmas: Holiday Adventures with the Doctor

Krampusproofing Your Home: Defensive Strategies for Yule

Silent Frights: A Collection of Christmas Creepypastas to Chill Your Bones

Santa Raptor's Jolly Carnage: A Dino-Claus Christmas Tale

Prehistoric Palettes: A Dino Wicca Coloring Journey

The Christmas Wishkeeper Chronicles

The Starlight Sleigh: A Holiday Journey

Elf Secrets: The True Magic of the North Pole

Candy Cane Conjurations

Cooking with Kids: Recipes Under 20 Minutes

Doctor Who: The TARDIS Confiscation

The Anxiety First Aid Kit: Quick Tools to Calm Your Mind

Frosty Whispers: A Winter's Tale

The Infinite Key: Unlocking the Secrets to Prosperity, Resilience, and Purpose

The Grasping Void: Why You'll Regret This Purchase

Astrology for Busy Bees: Star Signs Simplified

The Instant Focus Formula: Cut Through the Noise

The Secret Language of Colors: Unlocking the Emotional Codes

Sacred Fossil Chronicles: Blank Journal

The Christmas Cottage Miracle

Feeding Frenzy: Graboid-Inspired Recipes

Manifest in Minutes: The Quick Law of Attraction Guide

The Symbiote Chronicles: Doctor Who's Venomous Journey

Think Tiny, Grow Big: The Minimalist Mindset

The Energy Key: Unlocking Limitless Motivation

New Year, New Magic: Manifesting Your Best Year Yet

Unstoppable You: Mastering Confidence in Minutes

Infinite Energy: The Secret to Never Feeling Drained

Lightning Focus: Mastering the Art of Productivity in a Distracted World

Saturnalia Manifestation Magick: A Guide to Unlocking Abundance During the Solstice

Graboids and Garland: The Ultimate Tremors-Themed Christmas Guide

12 Nights of Holiday Magic

The Power of Pause: 60-Second Mindfulness Practices

The Quick Reset: How to Reclaim Your Life After Burnout
The Shadow Eater: A Tale of Despair and Survival
The Micro-Mastery Method: Transform Your Skills in Just Minutes a Day
Reclaiming Time: How to Live More by Doing Less
Chronovore: The Eternal Nexus
If you want solar for your home go here: https://www.harborsolar.live/apophisenterprises/

Get Some Tarot cards: https://www.makeplayingcards.com/sell/
apophis-occult-shop

Get   some   shirts: https://www.bonfire.com/store/apophis-shirt-emporium/

<u>**Instagrams:**</u>
@apophis_enterprises,
@apophisbookemporium,
@apophisscardshop
Twitter: @apophisenterpr1
Tiktok:@apophisenterprise
Youtube: @sg1fan23477, @FiresideRetreatKingdom
Hive: @sg1fan23477
CheeLee: @SG1fan23477

Podcast: Apophis Chat Zone: https://open.spotify.com/show/5zXbrCLEV2xzCp8ybrfHsk?si=fb4d4fdbdce44dec

Newsletter: https://apophiss-newsletter-27c897.beehiiv.com/

If you want to support me or see posts of other projects that I have come over to: **buymeacoffee.com/mpetchinskg**

I post there daily several times a day

Get your Dinowicca or Christmas themed digital products, especially Santa Raptor songs and other musics. Here: **https://sg1fan23477.gumroad.com**

Apophis Yuletide Digital has not only digital Christmas items, but it will have all things with Dinowicca as well as other Digital products.